RYAN
RnB
BARBER

WEIRDO CALHOUN
AND THE
ODD MEN OUT

written, produced, and rapped by

illustrated by Stu Helm

Eifrig Publishing LLC
Berlin Lemont

music by Snake Oil Medicine Show
& Yo Mama's Big Fat Booty Band

Published by Eifrig Publishing,
PO Box 66, Lemont, PA 16851, USA
Knobelsdorffstr. 44, 14059 Berlin, Germany.

For information regarding permission, write to:
Rights and Permissions Department,
Eifrig Publishing,
PO Box 66, Lemont, PA 16851, USA.
permissions@eifrigpublishing.com, +1-888-340-6543

Library of Congress Cataloging-in-Publication Data

  23 Skidoo, Secret Agent. Weirdo Calhoun and the Odd Men Out
written by Secret Agent 23 Skidoo, illustrated by Stu Helm

      Hip Hop Version: music by Yo Mama's Big Fat Booty Band feat. Ben Hovey,
         record scratches by Marly Carroll
      Bluegrass Version: music and vocals by Snake Oil Medicine Show
      Bedtime Story Version: music by Yo Mama's Big Fat Booty Band feat. Ben Hovey,
         Billy Jack Sinkovic, and Ellie Labar, vocals by Bootysattva

p. cm.

Paperback: ISBN 978-1-63233-006-2
Hardcover: ISBN 978-1-63233-007-9
Ebook: ISBN 978-1-63233-009-3

[1. Performing arts - Music - Juvenile Fiction. 2. Self-Esteem - Social Values - Juvenile Fiction.]

I. Stu Helm, ill. II. Title

18 17 16 15 2014
5 4 3 2 1

Printed on 10% recycled acid-free paper. ∞

WEIRDO CALHOUN
AND THE
ODD MEN OUT

TNFVJWGKBV

INSTANT AUDIO on your iPhone, iPad, iPod, Android device, or computer

This story is best when enjoyed with the funky music of Secret Agent 23 Skidoo. To listen to the track on your iPhone, iPad, iPod, or on any Android device, just search your app store for **stkr.it** and download the free app. Then just scan the QR code and the track will load. Or, visit **www.stkrit.com** on your computer, click PLAY, and enter the top secret 10-letter code at the bottom of the scan symbol to stream or download the music.

Don't forget to check the back pages for the Bluegrass Version, the Bedtime Story Version, and all three karaoke versions! You can rap, sing, or be a storyteller!

Between Chattanooga City and Kalamazoo,
By the Bermuda Triangle and Timbuktu,

Was born a little feller whose mom named him Sean,
But the doggone boy wasn't Sean very long.

The sun and the moon, they danced on and on,
But the doggone boy wasn't Sean very long.

When he started to walk, he danced instead,
 And when he started to talk, he sang what he said.

He fingerpainted secret code all over his room,
 And pretty soon they all called him Weirdo Calhoun.

He'd croon his own tunes till half past noon,
 And pretty soon they all called him Weirdo Calhoun.

Now some people worried 'cause they thought he was strange.
His clothes were always dirty and sloppy and stained,

'Cause he'd crawl and explore, and he'd run and he'd play,
But Weirdo Calhoun, he had fun all day.

In front yards and junkyards 'til the sun went away,
That Weirdo Calhoun, he had fun all day.

He got older and weirder and kept singing his songs.
  He'd make up inventions and bring 'em along.

Like his fine feathered space helmet, complete with snorkel,
  Weirdo Calhoun didn't try to be normal.

Thinking marshmallow pickle kabobs were tasty morsels,
  Weirdo Calhoun didn't try to be normal.

The bullies at school, they would call him a fool
    'Cause he wasn't popular and didn't follow their rules,

But he was thinking 'bout catapults and lock-picking tools
    Instead of whether or not they thought he was cool.

He was thinking 'bout a big jello-filled swimming pool
    Instead of whether or not they thought he was cool.

Now there are always kids that don't fit in the mold,
   And just because they want to act different they're told

They're a geek or a nerd or a spaz or a zero.
   It's really not that hard to get called a weirdo.

You could have a lazy eye or an extra long earlobe –
   It's really not that hard to get called a weirdo.

The other weirdo kids, they began to watch and notice
That Weirdo Calhoun, he just never lost his focus.

There were no words bullies could find to erase
The twinkle in his eyes and the smile on his face,

Like his mind was a million miles off in space,
With a twinkle in his eyes and a smile on his face.

They got together and began to hang as a gang.
   They grabbed pots and pans they would clang when he sang.

They'd sing along and yell and hoot and holler and shout,
   They were Weirdo Calhoun and the Odd Men Out.

Only the clouds knew what they talked about.
   They were Weirdo Calhoun and the Odd Men Out.

And this pack of strange kids had brains galore,
So their brainstorm ideas would rain and pour.

A tricycle paddleboat with a glass bottom!
Superfly crazy ideas, they got 'em!

Their potato guns made sonic booms when they shot 'em!
Superfly crazy ideas, they got 'em!

The same boring bullies still teased them in class,
But were they sad? There was no reason for that!

When you fly on kiddie pools filled with helium gas,
It's too fun to care if you're seeing them laugh.

Putting speed bumps on ski jumps to go medium fast
Is too fun to care if you're seeing them laugh.

One day some new folks traveled to town
  And told everybody to gather around.

They had big cars, big teeth, and suits and ties,
  And they brought along a super-duper surprise –

A contest with a prize too huge to describe!
  Yep, they brought along a super-duper surprise!

Now, these folks were Ad Men that sold cereal,
But their commercials had boring old material.

They needed some kids with some crazy thoughts
To be on a commercial for their Raisin Pops.

The most amazing kids got their face on the box
And got in that commercial for their Raisin Pops!

They'd have a competition one month from that day,
Where everyone in town got to jump on a stage,

And, whether they were graceful or their style was clumsy,
Whoever did a trick the most wild and funny

Won the grand prize and a big pile of money
For doing that trick the most wild and funny.

Dancers and singers started practicing acts
    While magicians practiced pulling rabbits from hats.

Gymnasts did back flips; no one thought about
    Weirdo Calhoun and the Odd Men Out.

Everyone saw themselves as winners, not a doubt!
    Even Weirdo Calhoun and the Odd Men Out...

The month just flew by, and it was time for the show.
The town was in costumes, all lined up in rows.

Skaters popped ollies, bikers did bunny hops,
And everybody wanted that money a lot.

There were yo-yos and tu-tus and real funny socks,
And everybody wanted that money a lot.

Everyone was called up by name from a long list,
    And, after ping-pong tricks and songs played on armpits,

They still hadn't seen Weirdo Calhoun's set,
    'Cause W is near the end of the alphabet.

They still hadn't seen the Odd Men Out's talents yet,
    'Cause W is near the end of the alphabet.

When their turn came, they all juggled tangerines
   While jumping on pogo sticks on trampolines!

And, while the tangerines went round and round,
   They also juggled red balloons upside down!

The balloons floated up; they hit 'em down to the ground.
   That's how you juggle red balloons upside down.

Then, erupting from behind the stage, the big finisher!
  A 10-foot volcano of baking soda and vinegar!

They pogoed to the top, then they snowboarded down!
  The cheering audience was heard all over the town!

A gasping and clapping crashing ocean of sound,
  The cheering audience was heard all over the town!

So Weirdo Calhoun and his gang won the contest,
    And got on the box and commercial, as promised.

But when the cameraman came to take some shots,
    They got one weird looking box of Raisin Pops.

The Odd Men Out just made faces and talked!
    It was one weird looking box of Raisin Pops.

They got that pile of money and decided to throw down
  And spend it on a party, then invited the whole town.

You could jump a snowboard off of a catapult
  Into a helium-filled kiddie pool that would float.

Or you could jump from trampolines attached to paddleboats
  Into a helium-filled kiddie pool that would float.

That night when the whole town lay in their beds,
    The most amazing dream-movies played in their heads,

And everybody ended up paying attention
    When they woke up thinking 'bout crazy inventions.

Some were crystal clear and some too hazy to mention,
    But everyone was thinking 'bout crazy inventions.

And over the years they made those ideas happen
    Until the town was full of all their minds could imagine –

Like the restaurant that served lemon-lime sauerkraut,
    Owned by Weirdo Calhoun and the Odd Men Out.

And everybody loved the peanut butter smoked trout,
    Cooked by Weirdo Calhoun and the Odd Men Out!

*The End

Bonus Video

YCRRPKDGWT

Simply search and download the **stkr.it** app on your mobile device. Then scan each **stkr.it** code to stream the song. You can also visit the website at **www.stkrit.com**, click PLAY, and enter the 10-letter code to stream or download the tracks.

TNFVJWGKBV

Hip Hop

HKNRSSFMQM

Bluegrass

GQCSYQLNYD

Bedtime Story

MYHPYKJPCW

Hip Hop Karaoke

HKLPCWXRWX

Bluegrass Karaoke

FDTPKDQJFB

Bedtime Karaoke

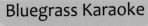

If you need a CD, they are available at www.secretagent23skidoo.com and at www.eifrigpublishing.com.

Celebrated as the "King of Kid Hop," Secret Agent 23 Skidoo is a one-of-a-kind, stand-out star in the indie family music scene. A proud father and stoked husband with a decade of experience nationally touring with and producing various hip hop acts, he joined his worlds together in a flash of inspiration and created a family hip hop band with his wife and daughter. Mixing sophisticated instrumental funk with intelligent storytelling and uplifting rhymes has earned them a large and loyal fan base, constant radio play, and loads of frequent flier miles while rocking stages internationally and having a blast!

"Secret Agent 23 Skidoo has married the complex beats of hip hop with the magical world of kids."   - Today

With numerous #1 hits on SiriusXM radio, a track on the 2012 GRAMMY-winning children's album, *All About Bullies ... Big and Small*, and gigs from basketball courts in the Bronx to stages at the Smithsonian, Lollapalooza, and the Winnipeg Folk Festival, Secret Agent 23 Skidoo is spreading the family funk far and wide.

"Through his music, he empowers kids to be themselves."
- USA TODAY

The core of the Secret Agent's mission is the celebration of originality and novelty, both in funky art and in quirky people. His songs and stage show are an energetic escalator to lift up the underdogs and let the light shine warm and bright on those who feel a little different . . . which is pretty much everybody. Armed with the belief that our differences are often our superpowers in disguise, he crafts beats and rhymes to spark inspiration in kids and families that trailblaze on the road less traveled.

"Witty lyrics and funky rhythms, smart yet fun ... a totally successful musical mission for Secret Agent 23 Skidoo."
- LA Parent

Deeply enthusiastic about language and the turn of the phrase, Skidoo has been a ceaseless proponent for reading and creative writing. He has created four years of music and lyrics for the US Library System's Summer Reading Program television commercials and has served as its official spokesman for New York State for two years. He has also developed a series of rhyme-writing workshops that help kids express themselves through the art of hip hop . . . which often results in the "class clowns" putting more focused energy into the assignment than anyone else!

"Nobody is making better 'Kid Hop' than Secret Agent 23 Skidoo."
- NPR's All Things Considered

Go to **www.secretagent23skidoo.com** for songs, videos, CDs, DVDs, tour schedule, booking, and to stay in touch with the premier purveyors of positive family Hip Hop!

Eifrig Publishing is bringing great music to kids!

Check out these other award-winning musical titles that both you and your kids will enjoy listening to time and time again!

Mixed-up Morning Blues:
Here is some great music by rhythm-and-blues artist Mark Ross, served up by a righteous twelve-piece band with a ton of help from "his kids" along with lively illustrations in an easy-to-follow book format.
Hardcover ISBN: 978-1-936172-13-9

Green Golly and Her Golden Flute:
A fun introduction to classical music with a Rapunzel-esque story, the silly storytelling of Keith Torgan, and the beautiful sounds of the flute by Barbara Siesel. Includes the 30-minute story track and 10 classical works performed on flute and piano.
Hardcover ISBN: 978-1-936172-62-7

Keep your eyes peeled for more funky family-friendly books from Eifrig Publishing!